MY FIRST B

KENYA

ALL ABOUT KENYA FOR KIDS

GL🌐BED
CHILDREN BOOKS

Interior and cover Design: Daniel Day
Editor: Margaret Bam

For My Sons, Daniel, David and Jude

Women carrying water in Kenya

Kenya

Kenya is a **country**.

A country is land that is controlled by a **single government**. Countries are also called **nations, states, or nation-states**.

Countries can be **different sizes**. Some countries are big and others are small.

Diani beach, Kenya

Where Is Kenya?

Kenya is located in the continent of Africa.

A continent is a massive area of land that is separated from others by water or other natural features.

Kenya is situated in the eastern part of Africa.

Downtown Nairobi

Capital

The capital of Kenya is Nairobi.

Nairobi is located in the **south central part** of the country.

Nairobi is the largest city in Kenya.

Maasai morans tribesmen in Kenya

Counties

Kenya is divided into 47 counties

The counties of Kenya are as follows

Mombasa, Isiolo, Murang'a, Laikipia, Siaya, Kwale, Meru, Kiambu, Nakuru, Kisumu, Kilifi, Tharaka Nithi, Turkana, Narok, Homa Bay, Tana River, Embu, West Pokot, Kajiado, Migori, Lamu, Kitui, Samburu, Kericho, Kisii, Taita Taveta, Machakos, Trans Nzoia, Bomet, Nyamira, Garissa, Makueni, Uasin Gishu, Kakamega, Nairobi City, Wajir, Nyandarua, Elgeyo/Marakwet, Vihiga, Mandera, Nyeri, Nandi, Bung'oma, Marsabit, Kirinyaga, Baringo and Busia.

Population

Kenya has a population of around **55.8 million people** making it the 7th most populated country in Africa and the 27th most populated country in the world.

Giraffes in Kigio Wildlife Camp, Kenya

Size

Kenya is **580,367 square kilometres** making it the 48th largest country in the world by area. Kenya is the 24th largest country in Africa.

Languages

The official languages of Kenya are **Swahili and English.** The English language is spoken by hundreds of million people around the world.

There are 69 languages spoken in Kenya, most belong to two broad language families: Niger-Congo (Bantu branch) and Nilo-Saharan (Nilotic branch).

Here are a few Swahili phrases and sayings

- **Hujambo** - Hello
- **Habari Gani?** - How are you?

Amboseli, National park, Tsavo West, Kenya

Attractions

There are lots of interesting places to see in Kenya.

Some beautiful places to visit in Kenya are

- Nairobi National Park
- Amboseli National Park
- Masai Mara National Reserve
- Tsavo East National Park
- Giraffe Centre
- Hells Gate National Park

Lamu Island, Kenya

History of Kenya

People have lived in Kenya for a very long time. In fact, fossils found in Kenya have shown that primates inhabited the area for more than 20 million years.

Kenya's earliest inhabitants were the hunter-gatherers.

Kenya gained independence from the United Kingdom on 12th December 1964.

Mount Kenya

Customs in Kenya

Kenya has many fascinating customs and traditions.

- In Kenya, many people only use the left hand for unhygienic acts. The right hand is used for eating and touching and passing things to others.
- Every contact between people in Kenya starts with a greeting. Shaking hands upon meeting and departure is normal between both men and women.

Nairobi Skyline

Music of Kenya

There are many different music genres in Kenya such as **Benga music, Genge, African popular music, Boomba music, Mugithi, Afrobeats, Taarab, Kenyan hip hop and Gospel music.**

Some notable Kenyan musicians include

- **Avril**
- **Sanaipei Tande**
- **Eric Wainaina**
- **Kaka Sungura**
- **Wahu**
- **Suzanna Owiyo**

Food of Kenya

Kenyan food is known for being tasty, delicious and flavoursome.

The national dish of Kenya is **Nyama choma,** a delicious seasoned barbequed meat.

Ugali

Food of Kenya

Some popular dishes in Kenya include

- Ugali
- Sukuma Wiki
- Nyama Choma
- Chips Mayai
- Mutura
- Githeri
- Mandazi

Mombasa, Kenya

Weather in Kenya

Kenya has a **pleasant, tropical climate**, however weather across the country varies dramatically. The highlands experience cooler temperatures while the coastal and lowland regions are characterised by warmer temperatures.

Ostriches in Nairobi, Kenya

Animals of Kenya

There are many wonderful animals in Kenya.

Here are some animals that live in Kenya

- Lions
- Leopards
- Zebras
- Buffalo
- Giraffes
- Elephants
- Rhinos
- Hippos

Turtle beach, Watamu, Kenya

Beaches

There are many beautiful beaches in Kenya which is one of the reasons why so many people visit this beautiful country every year.

Here are some of Kenya's beaches

- Kilifi Beach
- Bamburi Beach
- Manda Toto
- Nyali Beach
- Shanzu Beach
- Tiwi Beach
- Malindi

Market in Kenya

Sports in Kenya

Sports play an integral part in Kenyan culture. The most popular sports are Football and athletics.

Here are some of famous sportspeople from Kenya

- David Rudisha - Athletics
- Eliud Kipchoge - Athletics
- Hellen Obiri - Athletics
- Wilson Kiprugut - Athletics
- Nancy Langat - Athletics
- Linet Masai - Athletics

Famous

Many successful people hail from Kenya.

Here are some notable Kenyan figures

- **Wangari Maathai – Nobel Prize winner**
- **Lupita Nyong'o – Actress**
- **Jomo Kenyatta – President**
- **Mwai Kibaki – President**
- **Ngugi Wa Thiong'o – Author**

Mombasa, Kenya

Something Extra...

As a little something extra, we are going to share some lesser known facts about Kenya

- **Kenya is home to Africa's second-highest mountain.**
- **Kenya is one of the world's leading safari destinations.**

Narok, Kenya

Words From the Author

We hope that you enjoyed learning about the wonderful country of Kenya.

Kenya is a country rich in culture and beauty, with lots of wonderful places to visit and people to meet.

We hope you continue to learn more about this wonderful nation. If you enjoyed this book, consider leaving a review!

With Love

Printed in Great Britain
by Amazon

32987699R00027